# Seeding Faith

Keeping memory firmly planted
when we see the Hand of God

Written by: Cypress Ministries

## Seeding Faith

From: *To Seed A Soul* series written by Cypress Ministries

Copyright © 2011 by Cypress Ministries

All rights reserved. No part of this book may be reproduced or transmitted in any form or by any means without written permission of the author.

ISBN 978-0-9834135-3-0

---

Published by Faith Books Publishing (www.faithbookspublishing.com)
*Spreading God's Word and the message He lays on the hearts of those who are called to do His work in writing.*
"For as the rain and the snow come down from heaven and do not return there but water the earth, making it bring forth and sprout, giving seed to the sower and bread to the eater, so shall my word be that goes out from my mouth; it shall not return to me empty, but it shall accomplish that which I purpose, and shall succeed in the thing for which I sent it." Isaiah 55:10-11 (ESV)

---

Unless otherwise stated all scriptures are quoted in the New Century Version (NCV) and are taken from the New Century Version®. Copyright © 1987, 1988, 1991 by Thomas Nelson, Inc. Used by permission. All rights reserved."

Scripture quotations marked (ESV) are from The Holy Bible, English Standard Version® (ESV®), copyright © 2001 by Crossway, a publishing ministry of Good News Publishers. Used by permission. All rights reserved."

Scripture quotations marked (NKJV) are taken from the New King James Version. Copyright © 1982 by Thomas Nelson, Inc. Used by permission. All rights reserved."

Scripture quotations marked (NIV) are taken from THE HOLY BIBLE, NEW INTERNATIONAL VERSION®, NIV® Copyright © 1973, 1978, 1984, 2011 by Biblica, Inc.™ Used by permission. All rights reserved worldwide.

# DEDICATION

This writing is dedicated to our heavenly Father
who so often reminds me to
"Be still and know that *IN ALL THINGS* I AM GOD"

To His Son, who is truly the Author and Finisher of my faith,
and it is in Him that I am able to find strength each day,

To His Holy Spirit who teaches me, leads me,
and tugs at my heart when I don't know where to go.

When I stumble with "Who am I?" the Lord picks me back up with
**"Who has given man his mouth, and makes him deaf
or mute? Who gives him sight or makes him blind?
Is it not I, the Lord? Now go; I will help you speak
and will teach you what to say."**
(Scripture reference: Exod. 4:11-12)

It is in Christ's name that I give all glory to God,
who is the true Author of these words that I have penned.
I give thanks to Him for I am simply a vessel
and humbled that each morning when I rise
He gives me a heart for His Word to write down.
And so with a trembling heart, I simply say, "Thank You, God."

## Table of Contents

Introduction ..................................................................................... 1
   Section 1: Face to Face With God ............................................ 5
      >> Rainbow Answers From God .......................................... 7
      >> The Beginning of Something New ................................ 11
      >> Lessons Learned ............................................................ 17
   Section 2: The Lord's Help ...................................................... 21
A Heartfelt Thought ..................................................................... 23
   Insight ..................................................................................... 23
   Your Turn: Creating a Memory Stone ..................................... 27
About Cypress Ministries ............................................................ 91
To Seed A Soul Series ................................................................ 92

We write you now about what has always existed, which we have heard, we have seen with our own eyes, we have looked at, and we have touched with our hands. We write to you about the Word that gives life. He who gives life was shown to us. We saw him and can give proof about it. And now we announce to you that he has life that continues forever. He was with God the Father and was shown to us. We announce to you what we have seen and heard, because we want you also to have fellowship with us. Our fellowship is with God the Father and with his Son, Jesus Christ. We write this to you so we may be full of joy.
(1 John 1:1-4)

# Introduction

> **Our ancestors in Egypt did not learn from your miracles. They did not remember all your kindnesses, so they turned against you at the Red Sea. But the Lord saved them for his own sake, to show his great power. He commanded the Red Sea, and it dried up. He led them through the deep sea as if it were a desert. He saved them from those who hated them. He saved them from their enemies, and the water covered their foes. Not one of them escaped. Then the people believed what the Lord said, and they sang praises to him. But they quickly forgot what he had done; they did not wait for his advice.**
> **(Psalm 106:7-13)**

God promises not only to walk with us but also to go before us. He never leaves us to deal with life alone. The more we keep our eyes open for His handiwork, the more we will be able to see and thank Him. The more we believe, the more we will see of Him in our lives. Not because He is there more now than before, but because we are willing to believe that He is, that He does, and that He has, and that what we have seen isn't mere coincidence.

So often after reading God's Word, as we go about the day, the Lord will interact with us. He will give confirmation, He will work in our hearts and in our thoughts, He will open up the lines of communication in so many different ways, or even give us a complete change of heart if we need correction. And that is what this book has been created for: to be a special place where *you* can journal what the Lord has done in *your life* so that you will have a written record to be a memory that will be firmly planted for you to come back to visit over time. Plus it will be a keepsake for you to have to pass down to those close to you so that *you too* can be a witness to others of God's faithfulness and what He has done in your life. Let us not be guilty in the same way our ancestors where. Let us not make their mistakes in forgetting His mightiness and all that He does for us. Let us not be afraid to share it with others so that generations after us will know that indeed *The Lord is God*, and is a faithful God, and that He does walk with us.

Here's a suggestion offered to you: when the Lord moves for you, spend a moment thanking Him. The more we recognize His presence in our lives, the more our eyes will be opened. Many times in Scriptures it is mentioned that the people had eyes, but they couldn't see. These people were spiritually blind. Growing up in West Texas, sometimes I would be looking for something that *was right in front of me,* but I missed it. My grandmother would comment that, "If it had been a snake, it would have bit you." I was blind to what was right there. Let's not be like that when we are seeking God and miss His evidence that is right in front of us. Have you ever heard the saying, "You can't see the forest for the trees?" By all means, let's look at the trees. Sometimes God's answers are so simple or come to us in such a way that we pass it off as, "Oh, wow. Look at that, what a coincidence." My friend, don't be so quick to dismiss it. It's just possible that it could be a handprint from God.

## EYES WIDE OPEN

One morning in my prayer journal, I asked God to help me see Him in all He does in our lives. I asked Him to help me not to overlook any of His handprints in my day. I asked Him to help me to see Him in *even the smallest things*. That afternoon I picked up our youngest son from the Girls and Boys Club and when he got in the car he asked me if before we went home, we could go to our "tree." (This is a special place he knows that I like to go to sometimes to just sit and pray or be quiet.) So when we got to our spot, I asked him what was up. He totally amazed me, because in his youthful innocence, he said, "Oh, I don't know, I just felt like coming out here and sharing something with you and then thanking God."

So again I asked him what was on his mind. He said, "Well, it is really just a SMALL thing, in fact, it's so small…I don't know, I just felt like God helped me earlier at lunch…." Then he hesitated, thought about it for a moment, and said that maybe he was just being silly, and asked me not to laugh, but for some reason it had just touched him and he thought it was really a "God thing." He finally went on to share with me how he had eaten a big breakfast at his dad's that morning and hadn't been hungry at lunch so he saved some of it. Since he had done this, later he had something to eat with his friends during an unexpected snack time. No, I didn't laugh. *It was a small thing*, but in his eyes this small thing became a huge **"GOD THING"** and when I asked him why, he said, "Because I recognized it. I saw that even in this smallest, kind of silly thing, God's hand was actually in it, and He was helping me." Again I didn't laugh; in fact, I almost cried. I was so amazed at how God had decided to show me *He had been listening to me earlier*. And, he answered me. He opened my eyes to see Him in the smallest of things. I showed my son my prayer journal and what I had written that morning. He smiled and thought it was awesome that the Lord would use him as a vessel to answer me. And in the process, God showed us both something.

When we take the time to acknowledge and thank God for what He has done, when we can write it down with our own hand, later it is easier to recall and remember what God has said and done. Let us not be guilty of our ancestors' sins of forgetting God's wonderful deeds. Also, when we record it in our own writing, the traces of God's hand, then the enemy cannot come back and rob us of memories of God's faithfulness. So, with that being said, in the second half of this book, we give you a place to record your sightings of God's handprints in your life.

*At that time you will say,*
*"Praise the Lord and worship him.*
*Tell everyone what he has done*
*and how great he is.*
*Sing praise to the LORD, because he has done great things.*
*Let all the world know what he has done.*
*Shout and sing for joy, you people of Jerusalem,*
*because the Holy One of Israel does great things before your eyes."*
*(Isa. 12:4-6)*

# Section 1: Face to Face With God

**My people, listen to my teaching; listen to what I say. I will speak using stories; I will tell secret things from long ago. We have heard them and known them by what our ancestors have told us. We will not keep them from our children; we will tell those who come later about the praises of the LORD. We will tell about his power and the miracles he has done. The Lord made an agreement with Jacob and gave the teachings to Israel, which he commanded our ancestors to teach to their children. Then their children would know them, even their children not yet born. And they would tell their children. So they would all trust God and would not forget what he had done but would obey his commands** (Ps 78:1-8).

*Scripture says, my faith will help you, and your faith will help me, and that iron sharpens iron. In the following section I share with you as testimonies a few times that God has moved in such a way that not only I, but my family, could see that it had been a moment from Him.* "**I mean that I want us to help each other with the faith we have. Your faith will help me, and my faith will help you**" (Romans 1:12).

# Rainbow Answers From God

**When you first started praying, an answer was given, and I came to tell you because God loves you very much. So think about the message and understand the vision** (Daniel 9:23).

I always think of this verse when I think of rainbows. It is truly amazing the lengths to which God will go to answer our heartfelt prayers. This testimony is how God heard the prayers of my 12-year-old son and moved in a mighty way to answer him.

During the late spring of 2009 Devin, Mason, and Wyatt would stay for two weeks at a time with their dad. One Saturday afternoon, it was raining somewhat. It was more than just a drizzle but less than pouring, and every so often it would clear up and be just beautiful. Around four o'clock in the afternoon, Mason texted me, and what follows is our text messages back and forth to each other. I want to share them with you so you will understand how limited our conversation was, and then you can understand and appreciate God's work.

- Mason: Where are you?
- Mom: Home, why?
- Mason: Hurry, go outside!
- Mom: Ok, I'm outside, what?
- Mason: Do you see it?
- Mom: See what? Is it still raining over there? It's stopped here.
- Mason: No, it's clear, don't you see it?
- Mom: See what? I'm looking around, don't see anything.
- Mason: Up in the sky, there are 2 full rainbows, one on top of the other!
- Mom: Oh wow! No, I don't see them, where are they?
- Mason: Toward the mall, I can see them out my bedroom window.
- Mom: Oh no! I can't see past the high school. But I'm glad you can.

At this point I went back in the house and pulled out the vacuum cleaner. It was peaceful, I was thinking about Mason standing at his window, wishing he were here at home, but glad he was enjoying the view. He then texted me again:

- Mason: Please just stop whatever you are doing and go outside. Just stand still and close your eyes.

So I walked back outside and just stood in the fresh air and closed my eyes. In my mind I pictured his blue eyes, his blonde hair, and his smile. I just stood there and enjoyed a few moments of fresh air. He texted me yet again:

- Mason: Did you see it?
- Mom: See what? You told me to close my eyes.
- Mason: Oh, I was staring real hard at the rainbow and was asking God to let you see what I was seeing. Oh well, I was just hoping somehow God would put it in your mind so you could see it.
- Mom: Oh Sweetie!! That is so nice!! I didn't see a rainbow, but I saw your face! I saw you smiling! I love you!
- Mason: I love you too. Ok, well, talk to you later.
- Mom: Ok, thank you!! That was so sweet. I will call you tonight.
- Mason: K

I spent the rest of the afternoon cleaning, praying for my kids, asking God to please bring us the blessing He had promised, and just experiencing quietness. The next day, I stayed home and never heard from or talked to anyone else. It was kind of lonely, yet kind of peaceful. I went to work on Monday, and it was no big deal, no big day. I left at five o'clock to run some errands. About six o'clock, I was driving by my office on the way home and noticed that my boss had returned with some of the work crew that was coming in from out of the field.

On impulse, I stopped in to say hello and grab a folder out of my office. When I went out to the shop, my boss was there signing some of the guys in. I stopped and chatted with a few of them and walked over to my boss. He asked how I was doing, how the day had been since he had been gone that morning before I came in, and where my boys were. We visited and then I found myself sharing with him what had happened on Saturday with Mason and how sweet I thought his prayer had been.

My boss had the strangest look on his face so I was starting to feel a little uncomfortable thinking that maybe my sharing with him, in front of the guys, about Mason's prayer hadn't been such a good idea. After a second, he just looked at me kind of funny and asked, "This was Saturday?" I told him yes, that the boys had been with their dad at his apartment and apparently from the third floor he could see the sky out toward the mall. My boss started chuckling and said I should go out and talk to one of our truck drivers. The two of them had been out at one of the shop sites and had seen the two rainbows and our driver had taken a picture of them. I was amazed! So I went out to the bay and found him.

## Seeding Faith

Dear friend, you have to understand, this man is a really nice man, but he's tall and kind of big, with a long mustache, work boots, and a baseball cap. He's one of our truck drivers, a big burly guy, and not the kind of guy I would have ever thought of as a "rainbow picture taking" kind of guy. So I went out there and asked him, "You took pictures of a rainbow on Saturday?" He replied in a very Southern accent, "Well, hello there, Miss Kassie. Boy, did I! Pretty things! Wanna see them?"

At this point I still didn't know what to make of all this. So I asked him, "Yes, please could I see them?" He pulled out his phone and while I was waiting for him to bring them up I quickly told him about Mason on Saturday. He went on to tell me that he and my boss had been out on a site going toward the mall. He had looked up and there was an incredible rainbow, two in fact, one on top of each other, and that they had been very visible so he decided to take a picture.

I was really starting to get excited and was wondering if it was what Mason had seen. The driver finally was able to pull the photo up on his phone, and there it was! It was so pretty, the lower rainbow was almost full, and you could see all the different colors in it. The second rainbow was up a little bit higher, and one side was just starting to fade. This man had managed to move his phone up just enough so that pretty much the whole photo was of the sky and the rainbows. There was just a corner in which I could see some phone lines and down on the bottom of the photo it looked like maybe a tip of a rooftop.

I literally took the phone out of his hands! I stood there looking at it in amazement, mentally thanking God and thinking how happy Mason was going to be that I had seen his "thoughts"! As I was scrolling down the photo, I looked at the date and sure enough it was Saturday's date, but what shocked me was that the time on the photo was 4:20! All I could think was that at the same time my little boy was telling me to just stop, close my eyes, and be still --while he was praying that God would somehow plant the picture in my mind so I could see what he saw -- across town God was working up an answer to his prayers. At the same time Mason would have been praying, God was tugging at this truck driver's heart to take a picture of the rainbows! I quickly pulled my phone out to show him the text messages and the time that Mason had sent them to me. I was so glad I hadn't deleted them!

Then I heard our driver ask me if I had a picture phone so that he could send the picture to me, and he did! I couldn't wait to tell Mason! That evening when I got to call him, I said, "GUESS WHAT! YOU WILL NEVER BELIEVE IT!" and I went on to tell him about what had happened. He was so excited and wanted to know if I had received the picture. I told him I had and that I would show it to him the next day when I saw him.

Sure enough, the next day when I picked him up from school, the first thing he wanted was my phone. The look on his face was so awesome. He just sat there holding my phone and said, "Mom, that's it! That's what I saw the other day. That's what I wanted you to see!"

Dear friend, with tears in my eyes all I could do was say, "God answered you! But even in a more incredible way than you were asking. God gave me the photo of what you saw in a way that I could keep it and look at it any time I want. It just took a couple of days to get to me."

Mason sat there listening to me as he was looking at the photo. His reply was priceless. "Wow, I guess God really did answer me. I just didn't know it."

I am truly thankful for this face-to-face encounter with God's awesomeness. I am also very thankful that God answered Mason in such a way that he himself could see God's handiwork. I am so thankful that we both learned a lesson that day: sometimes God answers us in amazing ways, but sometimes they might be delayed a bit.

Just think, if I had hesitated about sharing with my boss about Mason's prayer, or if I had blown off going back to the office that evening, I would have missed God's answer to us. I can't help but think that sometimes God will answer us, but we have to obey in order to see the fruit of His work.

This makes me think of the time Jesus asked the crippled man on the mat by the pool if he wanted to be healed. The man said yes, but no one was able to help him. Jesus told him **"Stand up. Pick up your mat and walk."** (John 5:8) The man on the mat could have stayed there and thought, "Okay, I'm healed." But when he obeyed Jesus and got up and walked, he experienced the fullness of Jesus' blessings! But remember, he had to obey first.

Had I not obeyed what God was pressing on my heart to share, I would not have experienced God's blessing, and Mason would not have seen fruit from his prayer. I am so very grateful that through Mason's prayers, many people saw God's divine handiwork. God is truly amazing!

## The Beginning of Something New

Towards the end of May -- two years ago as I write this - the number *forty* started "echoing" inside of me. I couldn't get it off my mind, and in my spirit it just kept being moved in me. Now I know that forty is a biblical number and that many times this has been a significant time frame (example: forty days, forty years) for God's people, but I couldn't figure out why it seemed so important to *me* at this particular time in my life. *(I understand now that God was trying to get my attention.)* Friends kept telling me that it was because I was turning forty in a few months and that this was why it was so noticeable to me. I could have accepted this, except for the fact that turning forty really didn't bother me. So on June 1st I cleared my calendar, purchased a new prayer journal and started watching and listening for God's direction and "power verses" that seemed to speak very strongly to me while reading my Bible.

***Exactly forty days later- I lost my job!***
***Not thirty nine days, and not forty one days. But FORTY DAYS on the dot!***

---

Friday morning on July 10th after making the "dreaded phone call," to find out that, yes, my position at work was no longer there, I went and sat in my car at a church parking lot, not too far from the house. I looked in the rearview mirror contemplating where to go and what to do next. This place where I was at, is where I like to go periodically when I need quiet time to think, but isn't as far away from the house as my "special prayer place" (*My Tree*) is.

I wasn't as shaken up by this as much as you would think. It was unnerving, yes, but I also had a sense of peace inside, and after the past "whole forty days," I knew God was in this. I just wasn't sure how at the moment. However, the eruption that I had just experienced had been extremely unexpected and a little bit shocking. But after the dust had settled, I realized that God was saying, "I have plans for you, and if you won't move on your own, I will move you." When I think back, I am reminded that even the Israelites didn't want to leave Egypt at first. But one way or the other, God had plans for them, and leaving is what they were going to do! So when it came time for me to go on to what God's purpose for me was, He made sure that I moved!

The following several pages are a chapter from *"The Very Heart of Worship"* that I wrote telling about what happened following this very unexpected change in direction and over the course of the next several months, that I would like to share with you.

## GOD IS MY GUIDE

... So there I was on this Friday morning. I had already gone to a place where I had known for a while that they needed a manager, but the week prior they had found someone. I have to tell you that instead of being upset or worried, I was at peace. I didn't know where I was going or what I was going to do, but at that moment I was not surprised the position had been filled, nor was I overly concerned about my next move, which was why I was sitting in my "parking space." I was somewhere between praying and just talking to God. Every so often I would look in the rearview mirror at the traffic driving past on the main street behind me. Verses kept coming to mind:

*"Seek first the kingdom of God..."*
*"Be still and know that I am God..."*
*"For I know the plans I have for you..."*
*"Don't go away searching, stay where you are..."*

I remember sitting there, letting this concordance of verses filter through my mind. Again, I caught myself looking in my rearview mirror, but after remembering Lot's wife looking back and becoming a pillar of salt, I stopped. After a while, I drove down to a spot at the river that is very important to me and went and sat at my favorite place to pray, which is under what my children refer to as "my tree." And pray I did! I didn't so much pray for help, as I did surrender to God. Then I went home to spend time with my family. My thoughts were that it was a Friday and nothing could really be done at the end of the week, so I would wait until Monday and get a fresh start. Dear friend, I never had to. And this is the part of the story that I really want to share with you.

That evening it was brought up during a conversation with a friend that I should go back into business for myself, that I should start doing private bookkeeping for small businesses. I was totally against it, thinking there was no way, we didn't have the finances, the timing wasn't right... the list went on and on as to all of the "no's" I came up with. Then an interesting thing happened: my friend asked unexpectedly, what I would call it. Out of my mouth came "cypress." When I was asked why, and what was a cypress, I found myself looking around the room trying to see what in the world would have brought that word to me and out of my mouth.

## Seeding Faith

I had a fleeting image in my mind of the huge tree I was sitting under earlier while I was praying, but as I said, it was fleeting and so I didn't think much more of it. I went on to explain that down south where I am from, a cypress is a huge tree. As we were talking, the thought of "Cypress Bookkeeping" became more of a possibility. Before going to bed that night I got on my knees and prayed, telling God I didn't know what He was up to, or what He was doing, but I trusted Him, and if this was something I should consider doing, then I was willing, but He was going to have to bring it to pass.

The next morning I got up and made coffee for everyone, then went and sat down with a devotional I had been reading. It was a nice devotional, though I will admit that I now can't quite remember what it was about, but it referred to a passage in Isaiah 55. Now, I am no Bible scholar, but I am somewhat familiar with Isaiah 55; however, for the life of me I couldn't think what part of Isaiah 55 the writer of the devotional would be pulling from in reference to his topic. So, I went and got my Bible to look it up. Yes, Isaiah 55 was what I thought it was, but I kept on reading and in the last two verses of Isaiah 55 this is what I read:

> **"So you will go out with joy and be led out in peace. The mountains and hills will burst into song before you, and all the trees in the field will clap their hands. Large cypress trees will grow where thorn bushes were. These things will be a reminder of the LORD's promise, and this reminder will never be destroyed."**

I have to tell you, I sat there dumbfounded! I read it and reread it! There it was: "cypress trees." Now I am thinking and wondering, what are the odds of that? I was already convinced that this was a God thing. Nothing had occurred the night before to bring the thought of "cypress trees" to my mind and out of my mouth, so in my heart I was already reeling from this. Just to appease the skeptic in me, I went and did a word search. Keep in mind that there are over 31,000 verses in the Bible. So I chose the four most common Bible versions plus my own preferred version. I figured five times 31,000 verses is 155,000, so how many times would a word search of "cypress trees" produce results? *Seven times.* Out of over 155,000 Bible verses from these five Bibles, the phrase "cypress trees" only came up in seven verses. When I looked to see what terms where used instead, I found that in several places in the different versions it said "large pine trees" instead of cypress.

Not only did God give me the name, but He did it in such a way that "in my language" I saw it and understood it. If I had just read the phrase "large pine trees" you probably wouldn't be reading this now because I would not have thought anything else about it.

But you have to remember that when God is working in us, or talking to us, He will do it in a way or in a "language" we can understand. When God is giving us directions, He isn't going to speak Spanish to you if all you speak and understand is English.

If it had been one of my sons that morning reading the Scriptures, in their version Isaiah 55:13 says, "Large pine trees." They would never have thought anything of it. But, because I had been praying for direction and guidance and asking God, "What do you want me to do?" when He gave me direction, He also made sure that it would come up and be confirmed to me in a way that I would see it and understand that He had spoken. I often think of the sign above the cross when Jesus was crucified and how the same phrase had been written several times in different languages so that everyone there would be able to read it and understand it.

However, my story of God's divine direction doesn't stop there. After reading these verses and doing a word search, my mind started racing. By that afternoon, I had found a completely furnished office, with quite a bit of temp work along with it. By Monday, I was opening a checking account and was bonded. Two weeks to the day that I sat in the parking lot, I was sitting in my new office working. And life was amazingly good. For all of three and a half months!

For three and a half months, temp work kept coming. I was staying really busy, and I was convinced that God had put me in that office, doing what I was doing. But I could never get full-time assignments. It was just one temporary assignment after another and then it started slowing down until several months later I came to a complete standstill! I couldn't go this way, I couldn't go that way, and I sure didn't want to go backward, but there was no going forward either. In fact every time I would start to pray, the word "standstill" was what I kept coming back to. I kept praying and asking God for clarity. I knew that He had led me to it, I knew He had put me there, but I didn't understand and so I kept asking Him what the "standstill" I had come to was all about.

Then over and over again, everywhere I turned, every time I read anything, including sermons and devotionals, everything kept coming back to "health" and "healing," so I started reading about healing and health. Also Jeremiah 33 started becoming a major Scripture reference. Someone was always quoting something from Jeremiah 33, so one morning I decided to slowly and with openness read Jeremiah 33. What startled me was verse 6: **"But then I will bring health and healing to the people there."**

One evening, I downloaded a sermon to listen to while I was working on some things. I was listening but not real intently. The sermon was about Paul's imprisonment in his own home for two years. The pastor was talking about how active Paul had been and that his primary objective before this imprisonment had been about starting and planting new churches, so it must have been quite something for Paul when God had brought him to this standstill in his life.

As you can guess, this got my attention very quickly! Now I was listening very intently. In fact I rewound it just to hear those words over again! Yes, the pastor really said Paul had come to a standstill in his life! God had brought him to a point where he couldn't just keep going and going. But what others might have viewed and had even intended as an imprisonment, God was using for good. It gave Paul much needed time for rest and to physically heal. It also gave Paul time to write four of our New Testament books. Books that may not have been written had Paul not had the downtime his imprisonment had given him.

Immediately, I was brought to conviction! I knew what my standstill and downtime was about. A few years earlier I had started the rough drafts to this book you are holding and one other. But for many reasons, I was forced to put them down, and then aside, and after a while completely out of mind.

I spent several days in prayer about this and the whole "cypress" thing. I asked for wisdom and understanding and most of all clarity! Then it started becoming clear. God had brought to me and given me the name "Cypress" and I added bookkeeping to it and ran with it! God got me an office, gave me divine guidance, and even gave me a name, but then I went racing with it. I realized then that God was trying to do something totally NEW in my life, but I was trying to turn it into something I was familiar with. I was trying to take the leading and direction God was giving me and turn it into something I could do!

I quickly began to have a new appreciation for Joshua 3:1-5: **Early the next morning Joshua and all the Israelites left Acacia. They traveled to the Jordan River and camped there before crossing it. After three days the officers went through the camp and gave orders to the people; When you see the priests and Levites carrying the Ark of the Agreement with the LORD your God, leave where you are and follow it. That way you will know which way to go since you have never been here before. But do not follow too closely. Stay about a thousand yards behind the Ark. Then Joshua told the people "Make yourselves holy, because tomorrow the LORD will do amazing things among you."**

In looking at *God as our Guide*; there are several lessons here that I hope you are learning and grasping. Also, I hope that in sharing my story with you, it will help you to have confidence in the fact that (1) God does give us divine guidance, and (2) when God is ready, He will take you someplace completely new! But I also hope that in sharing my story with you that you will learn from my mistake in following too closely, so that *you* don't wind up in front of God and detouring from what it is that He is trying to do.

Just like the Israelites I had never been this way before, so I needed to focus on God. Yet Joshua told the people, not to get too far away from the ark, but not too close either. I understand both reasons now. I guess hindsight really is 20/20. If we don't stay focused on God and we get too far behind, then we run the risk of getting distracted and losing our way completely. But, on the other hand, if we follow too closely we run the risk of running out ahead of Him trying to do it our way and then we realize we've missed a step or even a turn!

I shudder to think of all I would have missed if I hadn't stopped to ask God for His counsel that Friday. Or even several months later, when things weren't working out as I had planned. I could have just assumed that I had "misunderstood." In fact I had several people ask the whole Eve question, "Now did God really say?" I could have, in my discouragement, decided that maybe this wasn't what I was supposed to do. But I kept looking back at my journal of the "Cypress trees" and what followed over the course of the following months.

If I have learned anything, it is that God is faithful and God doesn't lie. I knew there was no way that the name "Cypress" had just somehow come from me and by random chance it was in the Bible verses I was to read the next day. I did not imagine the furnished office and everything that fell into place over the next few days. And let me tell you, I strongly suggest that when God is moving in your life, you write it down! Journal it and pick up a few of your own Ebenezer stones to remind yourself, *"That thus far, God has helped"* (see 1 Samuel 7). You will need them. It's very easy for the enemy to rob you of your memories of God's faithfulness when you are going through struggles or unexpected battles. It's very easy for your shield of faith to become a mass of doubts when going through seasons that look like the dead of winter. But if you will journal your "God Movements," if you will write down the traces of God's hand that you have experienced, then it is easier to hold on to the truth of God's handiwork in your life during seasons of limited sight.

So when I came to what seemed to be a wrong direction leading right into a dead end, I asked God, "What is this all about?" Had I somehow misunderstood the direction He was giving me? Did I take a wrong turn? I knew that God had moved me to this point, but I didn't have clarity or understanding. Instead of throwing my hands up in the air and saying, "Oh well," I went to God and asked for counsel. I prayed for understanding.

I am so glad I did. Because what I found is that yes, God was moving me, and if I would just wait and spend some time at God's feet, I would see that He had some major plans. Not just for me, but my whole family. Sometimes we as humans think we constantly have to be "doing." We don't realize that at certain times the most important thing we really need to be doing is following Mary's example and sitting at Jesus' feet. Most often, when God wants to do something new in our lives, He will start off first with requesting that we spend a season of quietness with just Him. During these seasons, we need to take some time to just learn from Him and give Him a chance to come in and clean house, to let Him revamp some things in us, to restructure us, and most importantly, to heal or repair any needs in us before moving us forward.

---

## Lessons Learned

*Welcome back, now that you have read how Cypress Ministries began, I would like to share with you the lesson this encounter has taught me.*

As I write this now, it has been almost two years since I sat in my car that Friday morning. In fact, right now it is the end of May, which was about the same time two years ago when I was having the whole "FORTY DAY" sound off in my spirit.

Boy how my life changed! I have learned what it means to be dependent on God. I have learned what it means to truly TRUST GOD and step out in faith when He says to move. I have learned that God is faithful to provide when you are leaning on Him when nothing else makes sense. I have come to have a deep appreciation for the manna that God sent the Israelites each day, and let me tell you, He really meant it when He told them to take only what they needed for that day and then to trust that He would send supplies the next day. I now know firsthand what it means to pray, "Give us this day, our daily bread." But I have also learned that "bread" isn't always money or literal food.

To date, and by this July 10th-- the two year marker of when I sat in my car praying and asking God what was next... I will have finished writing four books!

Well, actually I can say I have written a lot more than that. I will have *four core books* completed.

- Two out of the four books of *"A Worshiper's Heart Bible Study Series,"* with the other two already outlined.
- The introduction book for the *"Reflections of His Heart,"* Journaling Guide Series, and three of the twelve monthly journaling guides outlined

- And, this one which is the introduction for the *"To Seed a Soul"* series. Plus, I have the other two books for this series outlined. In fact, you could say that in a very rough manner, they are almost finished. I know how they are to be completed, but I am again at a standstill, because I can't finish them until God moves and brings to fulfillment what I know He has promised to do. I have sat down many times and "mentally" finished them, but until God "brings it to pass," I am again waiting for Him to act.

What I have learned is that it truly does take courage "to stay the course." It takes staying focused on Him, who alone can lead you through some very rough waters. It takes a surrendered heart to step down from our own desires and really mean it when you pray, "Your will, not mine" and then let Him lead you through the dark.

I have also learned that it takes a heart that is committed and a willingness to obey one step at a time, to be able to finish once you have started. I have also learned, perhaps for me, one of the hardest lessons, which is **"You will not have to fight this battle. Take up your positions; stand firm and see the deliverance the LORD will give you, Judah and Jerusalem. Do not be afraid; do not be discouraged. Go out to face them tomorrow, and the LORD will be with you'"** (2 Chronicles 20:17 NIV). And, **"So do not throw away your confidence; it will be richly rewarded. You need to persevere so that when you have done the will of God, you will receive what he has promised. For, in just a little while, he who is coming will come and will not delay. But my righteous one will live by faith. And I take no pleasure in the one who shrinks back. But we do not belong to those who shrink back and are destroyed, but to those who have faith and are saved** (Hebrews 10:35-39 NIV).

I have learned that it really is "not by my might or my strength but by the power of the Holy Spirit'" (Zech. 4:6). And that it *is in Christ* alone that I can find strength when I seem to have none.

In John 6, Jesus told His followers, "The only work God wants you to do is this, to believe the one He sent." What I have learned is that, "believing" is hard work! No wonder He only gives us this one thing to do, because sometimes *it's all we can do* -- all we can handle. But, what I have also learned is that if we will just do this part -- our part -- God is faithful to do the rest. That what would seem impossible from a human standpoint, really isn't impossible for God when it is His will for you. I have learned that God really can, is able, and willing to do what they say "can't be done." I have also learned that sometimes *"time"* really isn't an issue, and that what can seem to drag on at such a snail's pace can overnight be accelerated when God's time is finally right. Read with me a portion of Isaiah 60 that the Lord has really shown me here lately.

> **The sun will no longer be your light during the day nor will the brightness from the moon be your light, because the LORD will be your light forever, and your God will be your glory. Your sun will never set again, and your moon will never be dark, because the LORD will be your light forever, and your time of sadness will end. All of your people will do what is right. They will receive the earth forever. They are the plant I have planted, the work of my own hands to show my greatness. The smallest family will grow to a thousand. The least important of you will become a powerful nation. I am the LORD, and when it is time, I will make these things happen quickly"** (Isa 60:19-22).

I have learned firsthand, that if you don't believe God the first time and take "that step," He will send you back out into the desert to circle around again. It is also amazing how He will bring you back to the very spot your faith faltered and lean down and say, "Let's try again."

I've learned that there was a really good reason He parted the waters *first* when the Israelites needed to cross over the Red Sea, but then waited until they put their feet in the water *first* before parting the water at the Jordan River.

You see, when we first start out, God knows that we need to see that He can! We need to see and know that He is just as mighty today as He was back then. We need to see and know that He does not, *and has not*, changed. But, after we have had a chance to walk with Him and spent time with Him; He brings us to the promise, He leads us right up to where we are going, and then He takes a half step back and puts us to the test.

- Will we remember what He has done for us?
- Will we believe that the one who has called us is faithful?
- Are we willing to take that one step of faith into the unknown *before* He parts the water (or removes the obstacle)?
- Will we walk up in faith and claim what He has told us, even if we can't see it?

Here again, just like the Israelites at the Jordan, we find that if we will just look up to where our help comes from and take that *one step* and "put our feet in the water", we find that God will come in and takes up the rest. And it really does start with, *"Lord Your will, not mine. Lord whatever You want, just lead me."* I have to tell you, God really does hold to:

**Then I will lead the blind along a way they never knew; I will guide them along paths they have not known. I will make the darkness become light for them, and the rough ground smooth. These are the things I will do; I will not leave my people** (Isaiah 42:16).

*Have a wonderful Journey!*
*And God Bless!*

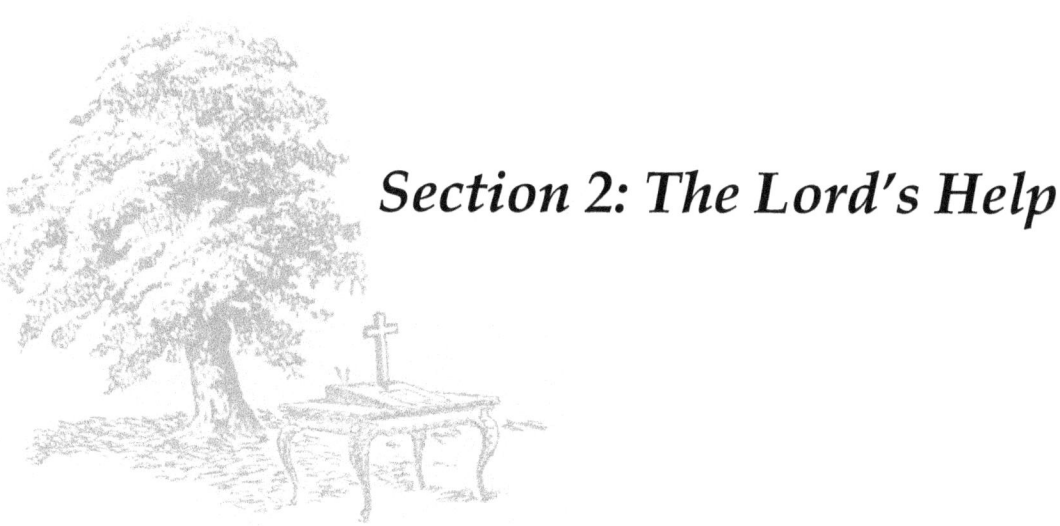

# Section 2: The Lord's Help

## ~ 1 Samuel 7:10-12 ~

(NCV)

While Samuel was burning the offering, the Philistines came near to attack Israel. But the Lord thundered against them with loud thunder. They were so frightened they became confused. So the Israelites defeated the Philistines in battle. The men of Israel ran out of Mizpah and chased the Philistines almost to Beth Car, killing the Philistines along the way. After this happened Samuel took a stone and set it up between Mizpah and Shen. He named the stone Ebenezer, saying, "The Lord has helped us to this point."

(NKJV)

Now as Samuel was offering up the burnt offering, the Philistines drew near to battle against Israel. But the Lord thundered with a loud thunder upon the Philistines that day, and so confused them that they were overcome before Israel. 11 And the men of Israel went out of Mizpah and pursued the Philistines, and drove them back as far as below Beth Car. 12 Then Samuel took a stone and set it up between Mizpah and Shen, and called its name Ebenezer, saying, "Thus far the Lord has helped us."

## A PONDERING THOUGHT:

When was the last time you took the time to pick up a memory stone to keep, showing those around you, and as a reminder for yourself that, *"So far the Lord has helped"*?

# A Heartfelt Thought

*"THUS FAR THE LORD HAS HELPED."* My friend, every day we need to remember that, "Thus far, the Lord has indeed been faithful." From the very beginning when God first said, "Let there be light..." He has shown to be faithful, mighty, and true. Only a Living God -- only a Loving God -- could forgive us for so much, and repeatedly offer to us His saving Grace. Only a God who can span the length of time, could see where we are today and call to us by name. He whispers to us and lovingly says, *"Child, you are mine."*

## Insight

In the passage of 1 Samuel 7, we read that Samuel had gone to the Israelites and had basically said, "If the Lord is truly your God, then follow Him with your whole hearts and lay down -- or better yet -- throw away all your false idols." (Read 1 Sam 7:2-3) And the Israelites did. They took to heart that the *Lord is God,* and they chose to follow Him.

While the Israelites were gathered, the Philistines heard about it and decided there couldn't be a better time to attack! But, what the Philistines failed to understand is that when you come up against a people of God's, then you come up against God Himself! The Lord told His people in Exodus 23:22, "If you listen carefully to all he says and do everything that I tell you, I will be an enemy to **your enemies**. I will fight all who fight against you."

When the Israelites saw they were under attack, they were scared and called to Samuel, "Don't quit praying for us!" And, Samuel didn't stop. He prayed through the battle. It says in verse 9, "He called to the Lord for Israel's sake, and the Lord answered him." The Lord being true to His word, fought for them. I love how verse 10 says, "But the Lord thundered against them..." My friend, when God steps in and goes before us in battle, it usually is with a "thunderous applause."

To commemorate the Lord's help, Samuel took up a stone and named it "Ebenezer," which literally means "stone of help." He used it as a visual reminder for the Israelites. My friend, if we will do the same, then we too, can give ourselves a visual reminder of a time that God has just stepped in and helped us. This aids in our walk of faith.

So often as time passes, memories will fade. You might have a brief mental image, but as life goes on and the next valley appears, it can be very easy for us to forget the grandeur of what just happened. It becomes an easy way for the enemy to taunt us. But, if we can keep a visual reminder, it is easier to remember the details of what happened. It gives us something to hold onto when we hit a massive storm when we are crossing into something new. It allows us to stand firm in our faith when valleys of difficulties are between us and a promise.

A Biblical example of God wanting us to "remember" I would like to share with you, is found in Matthew 16. Jesus' disciples were concerned because they had just realized that they had forgotten their bread to eat, so they were discussing it. In other words, they were worried, *but Jesus wasn't*. You will find in the passage I am fixing to show you, that there were two different conversations going on at the same time. Jesus was trying to warn His disciples that even the smallest amount of false teaching can easily spread, so beware, but the disciples where fixated on food. Jesus knew these men would need to eat, but He wasn't worried because He knew that somehow it would be provided. He was focusing on a different issue instead. He was trying to give them an important lesson. His disciples, however, were having a hard time with it so Jesus asked them, *"Don't you remember..."*

> <u>The Yeast of the Pharisees and Sadducees</u>
> **When they went across the lake, the disciples forgot to take bread. "Be careful," Jesus said to them. "Be on your guard against the yeast of the Pharisees and Sadducees." They discussed this among themselves and said, "It is because we didn't bring any bread." Aware of their discussion, Jesus asked, "You of little faith, why are you talking among yourselves about having no bread? Do you still not understand? Don't you remember the five loaves for the five thousand, and how many basketfuls you gathered? Or the seven loaves for the four thousand, and how many basketfuls you gathered? How is it you don't understand that I was not talking to you about bread? But be on your guard against the yeast of the Pharisees and Sadducees." Then they understood that he was not telling them to guard**

## A PONDERING THOUGHT:

In the passage of 1 Samuel 7, we read that before the Israelites went into battle, the Lord had gone before them, confusing the enemy so much so, that really the enemy defeated themselves. Has the Lord ever done that for you? Has there ever been a time that you were expecting a major confrontation, but when you got there, it wasn't nearly as bad as you expected? Or possibly much easier than you thought it would be?

**against the yeast used in bread, but against the teaching of the Pharisees and Sadducees** (Matt 16:5-12 NIV).

---

The next time God steps in and shows you a sign of His hand, I encourage you to write it down. Start a "Faith Journal." I'm not talking about a prayer journal; A "Faith Journal" is different. In a Faith Journal, you only write in it as you see God's movements in your life. Start by using a special color to write the "sighting," and then a regular black or blue pen to write down a brief message to yourself about why this was so meaningful. The reason I suggest two colors is so that when you're flipping through your journal later, you will quickly recognize God's movement from your own words. This becomes a powerful tool for you to look back at during turbulent seasons. When you can see something in your own handwriting it tends to help the mind recall just how it was the day you wrote it down. Not to mention, it becomes a wonderful treasure for your family.

Something else you can do, is to literally go get a stone. I have in our living room, a jar that contains fifty-seven small pebbles. One for each of the special memories that God displayed for me and my family during an especially difficult season we went through. During that time, I also took orange tabs and placed them at the bottom right corner of my daily Bible when I felt God's Holy Spirit highlighting His Word to me in a special way.

Now, whenever I look at those tabs – it is a reminder that the Lord did indeed help me through. Not only that, but He was faithful to do what He said He would do. For the rest of my life, those tabs placed in that Bible and the pebbles in that jar, will always remind me during other valleys to come – *"The Lord helped me then, and He will help me in this too."*

*My friend, the next time you hear a fabulous roar of thunder, close your eyes and just imagine that maybe the Lord is coming to fight a battle for someone who has laid down false idols and chosen instead to follow Him wholeheartedly ... Maybe it is someone you know, someone close to you, or just maybe -- that mighty roar of thunder is for you!*

**Have a blessed day.**
**Your friend in Christ,**
**Kassie,**
**from Cypress Ministries.**


### Praying In Faith:

*Father God, in Christ Jesus name, we come before you. Lord, thank You for the times that You have gone before us into battle. Thank You for the times that You stepped in and saved us from the enemy when we were not even aware of it.*
*Lord, we praise You for being mighty and able. Father God, we praise You and thank You for being our Lord God. Thank You for this day You have given us, and thank You that we can hold to the truth that so far You have helped us and that in the future, whatever it might hold, You will be there too.*
*In Christ Name,*
*Amen.*

# Your Turn: Creating a Memory Stone

*My Friend, may the L͟o͟r͟d͟ bless you and keep you; may the L͟o͟r͟d͟ make his face shine upon you and be gracious to you; may the L͟o͟r͟d͟ turn his face toward you and give you peace. (Num 6:24-26 NIV)*

The following pages are just for you. It is my hope and prayer for you that God will do amazing things in your life and in the lives of those around you, just to show you that He can, that He is able, that He hears you, and that He is with you.

**Memory Stones**

"Thus far the L<small>ORD</small> has helped us."

1 Sam. 7:12 (NKJV)

**Date:**

**God's Handprint:**

Seeding Faith

**Your Thoughts:**

**Father God, Thank You:**

### Memory Stone

"Thus far the L ORD has helped us."

1 Sam. 7:12 (NKJV)

**Date:**

**God's Handprint:**

Seeding Faith

**Your Thoughts:**

**Father God, Thank You:**

## Memory Stone

"Thus far the LORD has helped us."

1 Sam. 7:12 (NKJV)

**Date:**

**God's Handprint:**

**Your Thoughts:**

**Father God, Thank You:**

**Memory Stone**

"Thus far the L ORD has helped us."

1 Sam. 7:12 (NKJV)

**Date:**

**God's Handprint:**

**Your Thoughts:**

**Father God, Thank You:**

### Memory Stone

"Thus far the LORD has helped us."

1 Sam. 7:12 (NKJV)

**Date:**

**God's Handprint:**

**Your Thoughts:**

**Father God, Thank You:**

> **Memory Stone**
>
> "Thus far the LORD has helped us."
>
> 1 Sam. 7:12 (NKJV)

**Date:**

**God's Handprint:**

Seeding Faith

**Your Thoughts:**




**Father God, Thank You:**

## Memory Stone

"Thus far the LORD has helped us."

1 Sam. 7:12 (NKJV)

**Date:**

**God's Handprint:**

## Your Thoughts:

## Father God, Thank You:

## Memory Stone

"Thus far the LORD has helped us."

1 Sam. 7:12 (NKJV)

**Date:**

**God's Handprint:**

**Your Thoughts:**

**Father God, Thank You:**

> **Memory Stone**
>
> "Thus far the LORD has helped us."
>
> 1 Sam. 7:12 (NKJV)

**Date:**

**God's Handprint:**

**Your Thoughts:**

**Father God, Thank You:**

### Memory Stone

"Thus far the LORD has helped us."

1 Sam. 7:12 (NKJV)

**Date:**

**God's Handprint:**

**Your Thoughts:**

**Father God, Thank You:**

## Memory Stone

"Thus far the LORD has helped us."

1 Sam. 7:12 (NKJV)

**Date:**

**God's Handprint:**

**Your Thoughts:**

**Father God, Thank You:**

**Memory Stone**

"Thus far the LORD has helped us."

1 Sam. 7:12 (NKJV)

**Date:**

**God's Handprint:**

## Your Thoughts:

## Father God, Thank You:

**Memory Stone**

"Thus far the L ORD has helped us."

1 Sam. 7:12 (NKJV)

**Date:**

**God's Handprint:**

## Your Thoughts:

## Father God, Thank You:

## Memory Stone

"Thus far the LORD has helped us."

1 Sam. 7:12 (NKJV)

**Date:**

**God's Handprint:**

**Your Thoughts:**

**Father God, Thank You:**

## Memory Stone

"Thus far the L ORD has helped us."

1 Sam. 7:12 (NKJV)

**Date:**

**God's Handprint:**

Seeding Faith

**Your Thoughts:**

**Father God, Thank You:**

## Memory Stone

"Thus far the LORD has helped us."

1 Sam. 7:12 (NKJV)

**Date:**

**God's Handprint:**

## Your Thoughts:

## Father God, Thank You:

## Memory Stone

"Thus far the LORD has helped us."

1 Sam. 7:12 (NKJV)

**Date:**

**God's Handprint:**

Seeding Faith

**Your Thoughts:**




**Father God, Thank You:**

## Memory Stone

"Thus far the LORD has helped us."

1 Sam. 7:12 (NKJV)

**Date:**

**God's Handprint:**

**Your Thoughts:**

**Father God, Thank You:**

**Memory Stone**

"Thus far the LORD has helped us."

1 Sam. 7:12 (NKJV)

**Date:**

**God's Handprint:**

## Your Thoughts:

## Father God, Thank You:

## Memory Stone

"Thus far the L ORD has helped us."

1 Sam. 7:12 (NKJV)

**Date:**

**God's Handprint:**

## Your Thoughts:

## Father God, Thank You:

## Memory Stone

"Thus far the L ORD has helped us."

1 Sam. 7:12 (NKJV)

**Date:**

**God's handprint:**

**Your Thoughts:**

**Father God, Thank You:**

## Memory Stone

"Thus far the L ORD has helped us."

1 Sam. 7:12 (NKJV)

**Date:**

**God's Handprint:**

Seeding Faith

**Your Thoughts:**

**Father God, Thank You:**

## Memory Stone

"Thus far the LORD has helped us."

1 Sam. 7:12 (NKJV)

**Date:**

**God's Handprint:**

Seeding Faith

**Your Thoughts:**



**Father God, Thank You:**

> **Memory Stone**
>
> "Thus far the LORD has helped us."
>
> 1 Sam. 7:12 (NKJV)

**Date:**

**God's Handprint:**

**Your Thoughts:**

**Father God, Thank You:**

### Memory Stone

"Thus far the LORD has helped us."

1 Sam. 7:12 (NKJV)

**Date:**

**God's Handprint:**

Seeding Faith

**Your Thoughts:**

**Father God, Thank You:**

**Memory Stone**

"Thus far the L̲O̲R̲D̲ has helped us."

1 Sam. 7:12 (NKJV)

**Date:**

**God's Handprint:**

**Your Thoughts:**

**Father God, Thank You:**

## Memory Stone

"Thus far the LORD has helped us."

1 Sam. 7:12 (NKJV)

**Date:**

**God's Handprint:**

## Your Thoughts:

## Father God, Thank You:

## Memory Stone

"Thus far the LORD has helped us."

1 Sam. 7:12 (NKJV)

**Date:**

**God's Handprint:**

**Your Thoughts:**

**Father God, Thank You:**

## Memory Stone

"Thus far the LORD has helped us."

1 Sam. 7:12 (NKJV)

**Date:**

**God's Handprint:**

## Your Thoughts:

## Father God, Thank You:

**Memory Stone**

"Thus far the LORD has helped us."

1 Sam. 7:12 (NKJV)

**Date:**

**God's Handprint:**

Seeding Faith

**Your Thoughts:**

**Father God, Thank You:**

**Date:**

**God's Handprint:**

**Your Thoughts:**



**Father God, Thank You:**

# About Cypress Ministries

and Making JESUS' Name Known

*"For I proclaim the name of the Lord: ascribe greatness to our God. He is the Rock, His work is perfect; for all His ways are justice, a God of truth and without injustice; righteous and upright is He"* (Deut 32:1-4 NKJV).

First and foremost we seek, with all our hearts, to honor and glorify God with our lives in all that we do. It isn't about making us known, but to make HIM known. We have a deep desire to help others who are seeking to grow in their daily walk with God, while learning to listen to the leading of God's Holy Spirit; and simply coming to know God, to believe what He says and to worship Him, because He Is God.

*Following in God's direction, and the Pathway of Faith to spiritual health and healing.*

Cypress Ministries is the writing and leadership ministry of the Pathway of Faith foundation. Our main focus is on feeding those who are hungry (and thirsty) for a deeper relationship with God the Father (and the Way of Christ), through the teaching of His Word. Though our primary call is to "feed God's people" we have a deep burden as well, to bring a message of HOPE to the brokenhearted and downcast, to show them that all is NOT lost, and that through Jesus Christ there IS spiritual health and healing, and eternal life.

**For more information on Cypress Ministries or about our foundation, please visit us at**
www.cypressministries.com
www.pathwayoffaith.com

# To Seed A Soul Series

*We sincerely pray that the message we hope to express in this book has been insightful to you and has helped to deepen your relationship with God, His Son and the Holy Spirit.*

- Seeding Faith
- Growing In Grace
- When Faith Blooms
- Seeds of Faith 52 Week Devotional

*If you would like more information on this series,
our daily study devotionals, or any of our other Bible study series,
please visit our website at: www.cypressministries.com*

---

*In following Jesus' example, we are searching for God's lost people;
ministering to the disappointed, the hurt, and the lonely,
and gently reminding them that Jesus is the way.*

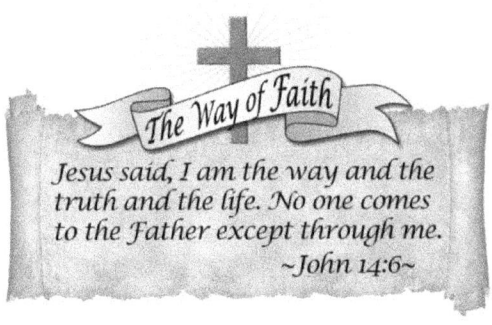

*The Way of Faith*

*Jesus said, I am the way and the truth and the life. No one comes to the Father except through me.*
~John 14:6~

www.ingramcontent.com/pod-product-compliance
Lightning Source LLC
Chambersburg PA
CBHW081016040426
42444CB00014B/3237